There's a Spider in my Bath!

Hannah Titania Middleton

Har-Ya'ar Books

There's a Spider in my bath!

Hannah Titania Middleton

Har-Ya'ar Books

There's a spider in my bath,
but it's one I'd never squash.
I wouldn't really mind it
but I think I need a wash.

I don't know when she's leaving,
nobody can tell.
I hope she doesn't take too long
'cause soon I'll start to smell!

Every time I move her
she always gets back in,
and no matter where I move her to
she never says a thing!

I see her climbing sometimes,
is she trying to get out?
She went there in the first place
so what's the fuss about?

4

I don't know why she does it,
she must be rather dim . . .
sitting in a bath all day
when she can't even swim!

I don't know why she likes it,
a bath can be quite deep
and to an itsy bitsy spider
it must be awfully steep.

So, today I asked my teacher,
Miss Webster,"Do you know,
why some spiders like the bath
and how to make them go?"

"Spiders get quite bored, my dear,
of catching flies all day,
the bathroom makes the perfect place
where spiders like to play.

Sliding down the sides of baths
is how they have their fun,
but sometimes they forget the bath
is where the bath is run!"

My teacher asked a question,
which really made me think . . .
"Why are spiders in the bath
but never in the sink?"

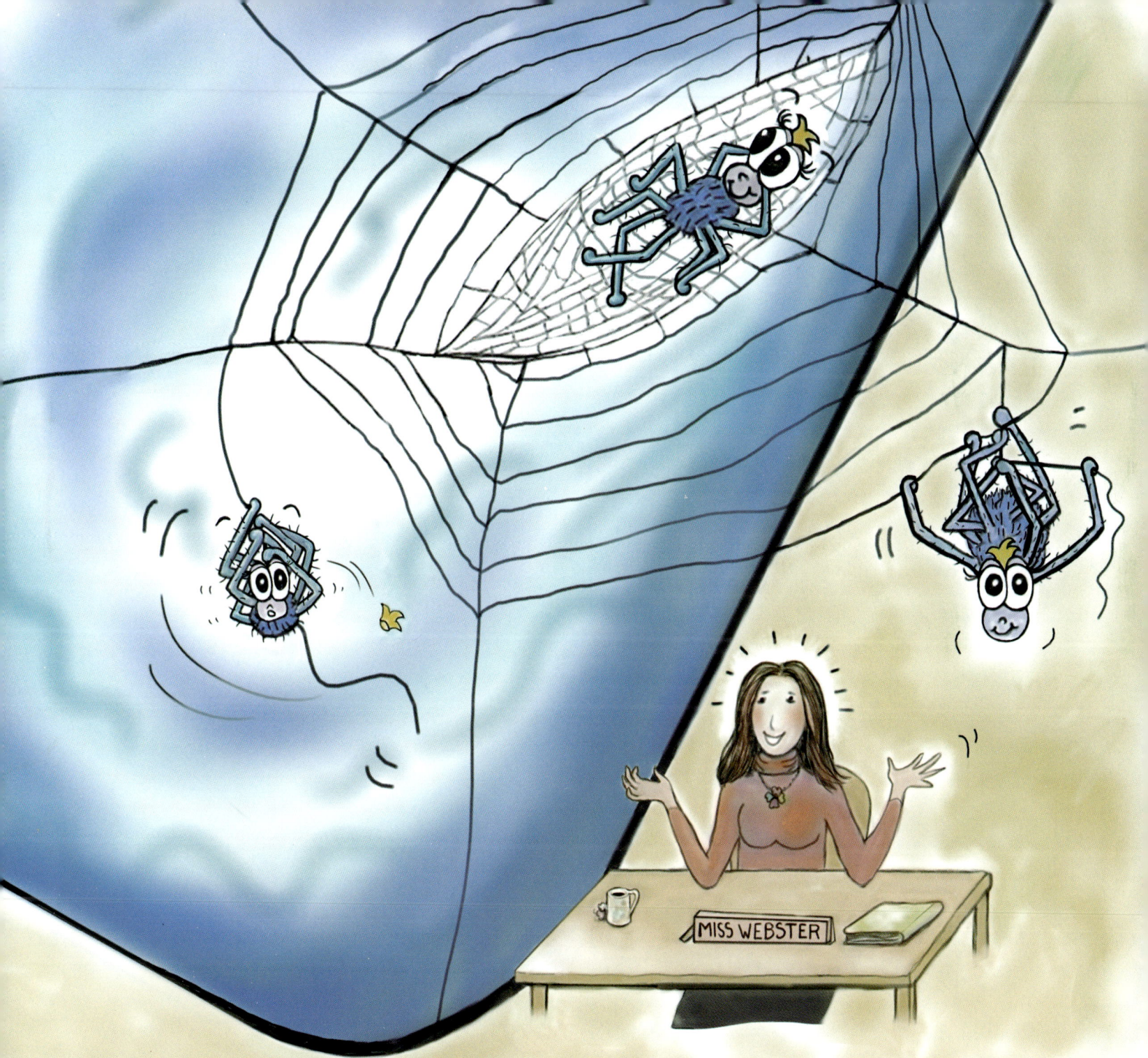

I didn't know the answer
so I asked her if she knew,
why spiders end up in the bath
but never down the loo?

She looked at me quite strangely,
and it made the whole class laugh.
She said "If I were a spider
I would always choose the bath!"

BEST TEACHER
AWARD

MISS WEBSTER

ASK ME
MISS WEBSTER
I KNOW
WHY!

My friend's mum's got a bug spray,
it says '<u>KILLS</u>' right on the side!
I could never hurt my Itsy,
there's a wee heart deep inside.

I put my hand beside her
and watched as she crawled on,
but as I started walking,
I realised she was gone!

So if I were a spider,
where would I want to go?
It doesn't really matter
'cause I don't think spiders know.

12

Well, luckily I found her,
hanging from my thumb.
I put her in a see-through glass
then showed her to my Mum.

Mum said I couldn't keep her
and I'd have to let her go.
She never asked my spider,
she might *like* the glass you know!

Well Mum just would not listen.
I suppose that she was right.
After all we've got no spare beds,
so Itsy couldn't stay the night!

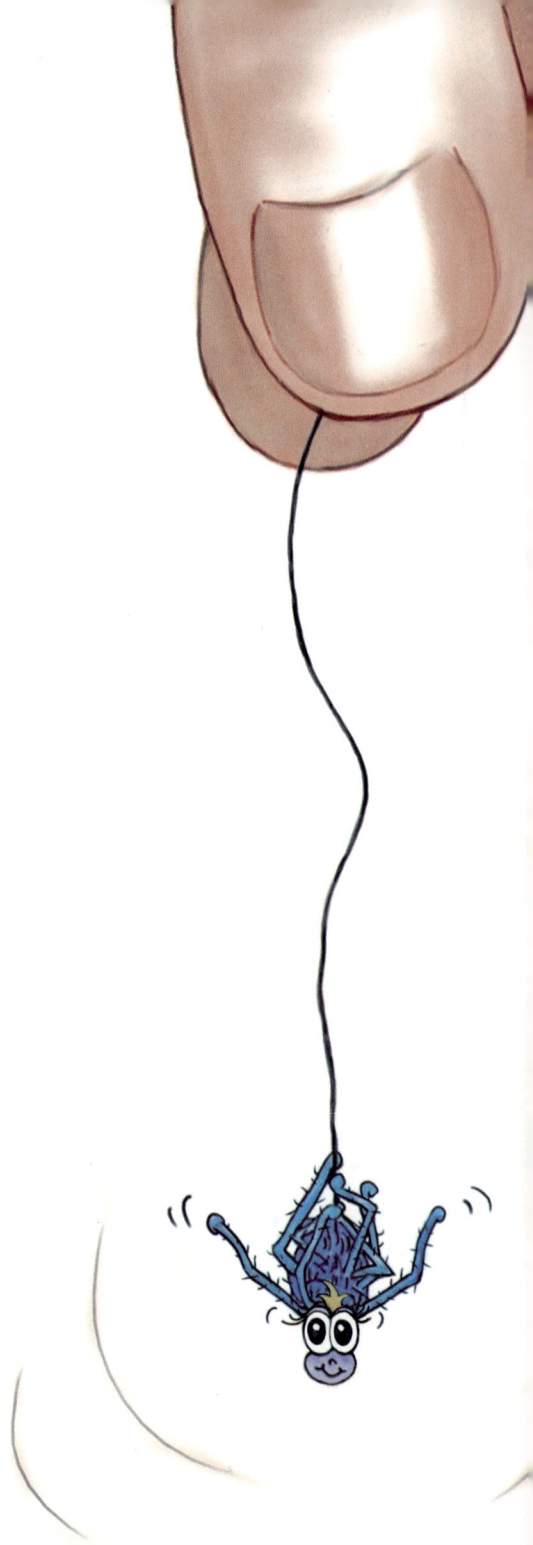

14

I took her to the garden,
'cause that's where spiders stay.
She was a good wee Itsy,
she was quiet all the way.

I placed her by a flower,
and then I said goodbye,
my Itsy she said nothing
- on account of being shy.

As I closed the kitchen door,
I watched her crawl away.
I hoped that she was listening
when I told her she could stay.

I watched her from the window
while Mum made us some tea,
then I began to miss her
and I'm sure that she missed me!

I couldn't help but wonder,
whilst stepping on the stair,
"Now bathtime might be lonely
'cause my Itsy isn't there!"

To get there from the garden,
would surely need a map,
but sure enough I saw her . . .

. . . waving from the tap!

I don't know how she did it,
I shouldn't really care,
I can't help thinking how on earth
she'd climbed up every stair!

She must have walked quite quickly,
she couldn't even wait,
her legs must help her somewhat
after all she has got eight!

Itsy bitsy spiders
are not that hard to find,
but MY little Itsy. . . well

she's one of a kind!

Now she never leaves the bathroom,
she's there come rain or shine,
but I don't really mind it. . .
just as long as she is mine.

Some kids, they are afraid of her,
I really don't know why,
'cause I know my little Itsy
and she wouldn't hurt a fly!

Hannah Titania lives by the sea in an ancient woodland on the remote island of Islay off the West coast of Scotland.

There's a Spider in my Bath!

Text and Illustrations: Hannah Titania Middleton

Graphic editing: Josiane Habib-Mor

Design and layout: Ran Levy-Yamamori

Har-Ya'ar Books

Environment, nature and us

POB 181, Binyamina, Israel 30500, Telefax: +972-4-6380039

email: ran@levy-yamamori.com

www.naturesaving.com

Address in Scotland, UK: Ardimersay House,
Kildalton, Port Ellen, Isle of Islay
Argyll, Scotland, PA42 7EF, UK